UCC Library, University College Cork

A Table of Books in Ballybeg

September 15th – January 10th

Coracle 2023

A Table of Books in Ballybeg gathers most of the Irish projects produced by Coracle, a small publishing press working from the townland of Grange, west of Clonmel in County Tipperary, between 1997 and the present day. Coracle has been producing books and other printed artifacts displaced from the page, often leading to installations for walls and other settings.

The Print Shed, with old number plates of past vehicles, and a disused pizza paddle.

In 1996, at the end of a second residency at The Irish Museum of Modern Art, we walked the largely unmarked St. Declan's Way over the Knockmealdown Mountains, down into the fertile valley beyond them. There we found the scattered compound of buildings that were to become our home. We decided to move to Ireland. In 1997, we went to claim the house from the farmer who had first shown it to us.

In contemporary life and language, it seems that the word dwelling defines almost the opposite of its original meaning from old English. Then *dwellan* suggested being led astray, delaying, tarrying for a while, wandering from the path. In spite of the rains of that early spring, we had loved the quiet isolation and dishevelledness of Ireland. Upon deciding to tarry for a while we felt that we had one house left in us to build and alter, and along with the ongoing work of the books, and indeed, how to live, we thought this a great chance for a fundamental change from London.

So we came accidentally to this hidden part of rural Ireland. We were not necessarily looking for a place to move but after bookshops and galleries made in a variety of places, we were seeking a project that would unify and integrate our production as artists and publishers with a place where this could be done: a fresh space with multiple buildings that we could adapt to our needs.

For six or seven years we built and repaired, improvising solutions to problems we had never anticipated. We made our buildings warm and watertight, cut our way through the tunnel of foliage which lines the dirt track to the house, and appended texts to some of the walls. A wooden tower was erected to be able to view the Galty Mountains, both as a distraction from the main task of house-building in the early days, but also maintaining that in the land of Yeats all poets should have a tower.

With the accumulated backlist of Coracle, some of which had by now become quite rare, and with the modest production of four to six new books a year, we could survive from such a remote place. Along with space and time, Ireland does not levy VAT (Value Added Tax) on books and to this day still maintains a special book postal rate at the Post Office, and along with a tax exemption for the work we made as artists, we felt certain we could live well below the radar.

These many years later we sometimes feel the need for a different integration: travel, the city, streetlights, and food we don't have to cook ourselves. The winters are long and dark and wet. But essentially,

The Print Shed platform

Cutting hay in the surrounding fields

publishing remains the same as always: the conceived book, its editing and production, its warehousing and distribution. For Coracle, very little fits an existing format, and each printing project presents its own problems. Or more fundamentally, as the American poet Charles Olsen said: *Don't ever be intimidated by the disdain and disinterest in the world. Get yourself some type, get yourself some paper and print it.*

We told ourselves that if we can publish from here, it can be done anywhere.

An addition to our activity in Ireland during this period of house reconstruction was the installation of *Vinyl* made in the Christian Brothers' School, Sullivan's Quay, Cork, during July and August of 2005, as part of the Cork City of Culture year. Contributions were made by thirty-three invited artists and writers using vinyl film as sign and graphic output from the computer plotter and cutter. This single means of production produced a common medium, creating a theme of material use. For the most part, it was a textual and graphical project, interspersed with uses of vinyl as a more purely inert material, used by some of the participants to build and construct.

Vinyl was essentially a project for an expanded book of parts, an anthology using the nooks and crevices of a building in an advanced state of decay, instead of the page. The works were layered onto existing surfaces, prominent features, and other facets of the building, their presence left to be discovered whilst situated in a collective space normally used for a different purpose: a school on Sullivan's Quay.

A central feature of the installation was a well-stocked book room made in the games room above the gymnasium in the building overlooking the river, focusing information on this and other projects, and books were available both for perusal and for purchase. It presented books by poets, artists and writers involved in the project, together with the work of Soundeye's Cork International Poetry Festival which shared the space in the first weeks of the *Vinyl* installation. The book room was seminal in its offering of the kind of books Coracle produces, perhaps to a new audience, as well as books from publishers from across Europe and beyond.

We have tried to avoid falling into the traps and platitudes of undue patronage of our adopted domicile whilst at the same time acknowledging a freshness and lightness of touch from our new surroundings. In turn we have produced collaborations with others, and with institutions, confirming that this is a way

The Bookroom at the *Vinyl* installation, 2005

Cupboard doors, with Maud Cotter corrugated paper sculpture at the top, a Gaudier-Brzeska toy reproduction underneath, the top of an early work by Roger Ackling, and to the left a facsimile card of *The Allies* cover used as an invitation to the exhibition 'Certain Trees' in 2008, all in the shadow of chalk chess pieces, above on a beam.

of breaking our isolation while participating in a dialogue of books, catalogues, invitation cards and other printed items. Amongst these are our first ever excursions into the editorial design for the crafts, working with artist and curator Brian Kennedy with *Of Colour In Craft* 2002, *Forty Shades of Green* 2006, *Material Poetry* 2010, *Dubh* 2012.

Collaborations with individual artists allowed us to engage with formats we were very familiar with and wanted to extend. The reproduced notebook has always held a particular fascination for us, and its use as a synthetic facsimile has been used in the following: Rob Smith *Views from a Windy House*, IMMA 1994. Alice Maher *Necklace of Tongues*, Butler Gallery 2000. The Notebooks of Thomas Cuddihy: *Boats, Cots, Punts and Wherries*, Workman's Boat Club, Clonmel 2004. Katie Holten *Notional*, Butler Gallery, 2004. *A Little Bit of Butter*, Cork Butter Museum 2007.

In a way all our books are a collaboration with their subject, no matter what authorship or editorial they come under, like Erica Van Horn's *Small Houses: The Buildings of Tom Brown*, 2007. Each tells a story, either anecdotally or more abstractly, and this is especially true in the writings of Van Horn. She has often worked in serial form. It was inevitable that she would develop from her *Italian Lessons* (made while living in Italy in 1990 to the *Living Locally* series of her Irish habitation. This series begins to incorporate the eponymous on-line journal, begun in 2007 and continued today, and the printed items of books, pamphlets, cards and postcards numbered sequentially in the series as they occur.

Some of the books made during this period are small, copy-shop editions, as there always have been, produced by xerox, laser and inkjet, often with the local printer-stationer. Van Horn's small-format books, like *Rusted* 2004, *Gifts from the Government* 2007, *Bus* 2014, and *Natural Cheese* 2015, amongst others, were lessons in finding direct ways to use simple photographic covers, reduced drawing and tipped-in imagery, all hand-stitched in the long dark winter months. These books were produced with modest processes, sometimes with a title line of coloured letterpress added from the small Adana printing press in the shed.

More elaborate editions were produced by large trade printers and binders, on occasion printed letterpress and hand-bound, not particularly for any craft reason, but because it was what we knew was to hand. Sometimes an entire production was completed by specialist book printers, like Peter Downsbrough's *Cork City* 2017, Erica Van Horn's *Too*

Group of book-aligned objects on a windowsill: two alabaster trials for *The Manifestation of the Poem / The Manifestation of the Book*, 2011; wooden arabesque by Martin Fidler, 1971; glass plate for Art Lyford, 2011; and 'transparency / translucency' glass poem, 1997

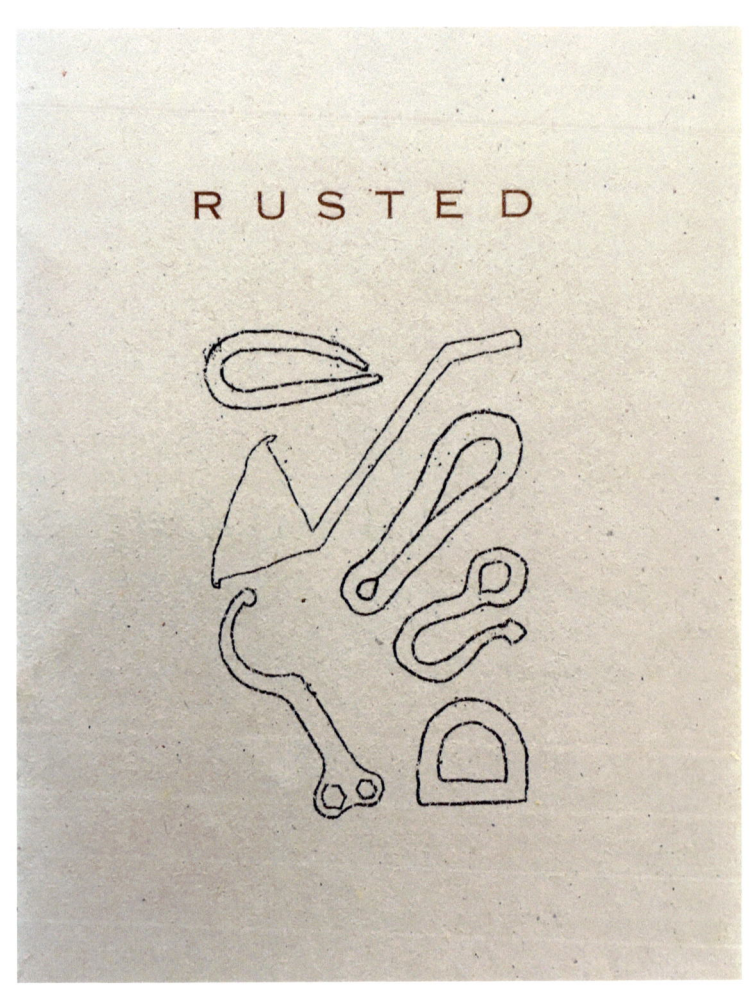

Erica Van Horn, *Rusted*, 2004

Raucous for a Chorus 2018 and *My Ironmongery* 2015, many of these typeset and produced by our friend Colin Sackett.

There have always been items of printed and found ephemera surrounding the general thrust of Coracle work: scatterings of postcards, folded cards, invitations to events, book prospectuses sent in advance, small format prints, like Simon Cutts *Struggle of the Fly in Marmalade* 2018, and Erica Van Horn *Springs & Coils* 2019.

For the UCC Library at University College Cork we have chosen to exhibit several new as well as some already seen projects. These may need a few more descriptive pointers to give them context.

14 Blackthorns began with the discovery of a bundle of blackthorns sticks tied with string in the sub-soil of what is now our main workshop barn. We assumed that these sticks were packed together to go to market for trading or to be sold. Erica Van Horn drew them as silhouettes and we printed the metal blocks made from them by letterpress, to exemplify their tactility with a bite to the page. The book is a collection of poetry, in a small but tall thin volume, the height of the sticks and the poems accompanying one another throughout its pages. A fifteenth drawing was embossed onto the spine of the book. Later, the fourteen became the print *15 Blackthorns*, 1999, when we added the last block. The actual blackthorns themselves have been used in installations in several places, but this is the first time we have used them as vinyl images with a text line underneath.

Folded Napkins is a small book from 2006, of images of napkins folded by visitors so they can remember which napkin is their own over several days of eating at the table. Here we have made the cover image of that book and this catalogue into a tablecloth and napkins.

The Money Jar 2002 was both a celebration and a lament for the end of Irish coins and the beginning of the Euro. The coins, with their birds and animals, were beautiful and distinctive. It seems important to us to mark their passing as currency. And as pounds and inches were replaced by metric measures the one pound jam jar was also being discontinued. We saved them, and weighed the jars. We counted the coins, seeking humble ways of remembering them even as they were becoming extinct.

Small Houses: The Buildings of Tom Brown is a project from 2007 which has been shown on many occasions, but is here used to focus on the place of our activity. The text on the gable-end of Tom

Invitation card, Cashel Cultural Festival, 2002

Joan Roth, *Four Trees*, 2017
"O Chestnut tree, great rooted blossomer." W. B. Yeats

Brown's model house is a replica of that at the end of our actual building.

Erica Van Horn, *My Ironmongery* 2015, is a collection of metal forms found around the buildings in Ballybeg, seemingly classified and numbered as in a catalogue of themselves. The printed drawings are then enlarged, mounted and hung in sequence as an installation, the page transfered to the wall. *A Soft Day*, the five photographic digital prints of cows moving in the rain taken through the car windscreen is a new work from Erica Van Horn, an extended version of her books *I always have an audience for my work, 1 & 2*, 2015 and 2019. Their still presence as print, paper and surface is in contrast to their turning as pages.

Four Trees 2017, the originals of which are now in the collection of the UCC Library at the University of Cork, for Coracle represents a small gesture towards the contribution William and Joan Roth made to the life of the arts in Ireland over many years. In the last decades of her life, Joan Roth established the remarkable process by which she completed her photo-drawings, finishing the bromide coated and exposed sheets of hand and mould-made paper with texture, shading and over-drawing from a graphite pencil.

At the same time most of the Irish-inclined books and ephemera will be available on the large table, and some scarce work shown in vitrines.

It has been a great pleasure to work with Crónán Ó Doibhlin, Head of Collections at the University College Cork Library and to continue this productive dialogue. It has always been our intention to draw up an Irish list of books and printed items produced and relating to our life here to date, and this exhibition has given us the opportunity.

Simon Cutts & Erica Van Horn
Coracle 2023

Erica Van Horn, *A Soft Day*, 2023

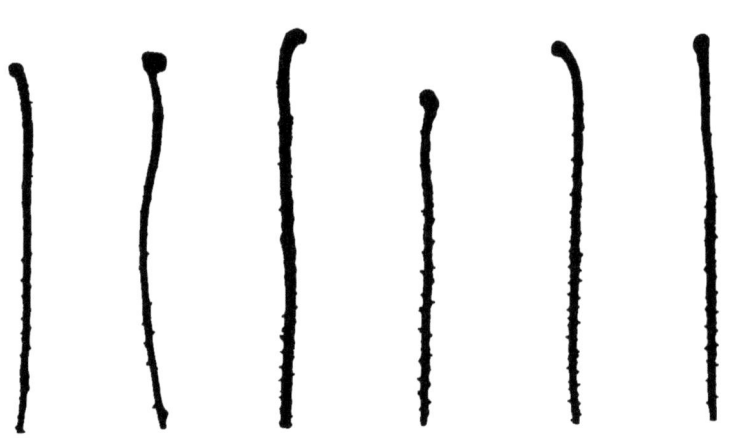

14 blackthorns, their root & sap fruited not t

oes but the occasion of climbing the path

The Irish Harp: proposal for a neon
Simon Cutts, 2023
12pp 165 x 120, digital, wire stitched, with text line wrapper over cover.

of Lichen & Moss
drawings by Kate Van Houten, writings by Erica Van Horn, 2022
32pp 125 x 140, digital, casebound paper over boards.

A Table in Ballybeg
Simon Cutts & Erica Van Horn, 2021
64pp 185 x 145, colour offset, casebound paper over boards.

Unique Forms of Continuity in Space
Simon Cutts & Maud Cotter, 2020
36pp 175 x 150, casebound picnic paper over boards, with embossed cover image, and seven tipped-in images of the series.

Domestic Interior
Simon Cutts & Erica Van Horn, 2021
170 x 135, folded card, letterpress, with cotton appendages, in envelope

Living Locally series 2002–2019
Erica Van Horn, 2020
The complete series of 32 items, books, pamphlets, cards in box 27 x 19 x 6.
No.1-8 *Some Words For Living Locally*, 2002; No.9 *Chaynie*, 2005; No.10 *against mice burn sage*, 2007; No.11 *Gifts from the Government*, 2007; No.12 *Small Houses: The Buildings of Tom Browne*, 2007; No.13 *Eight Old Irish Apples*, 2008; No.14 *Rosemary*, 2008; No.15 *Weather Forecast*, 2008; No.16 *Rain*, 2009; No.17 *Eight Old Irish Potatoes*, 2011; No.18 *Some More Words For Living Locally*, 2011; No.19 *A Hot Drop*, 2012; No.20 *Elderflower*, 2012; No.21 *Born in Clonmel*, 2012; No.22 *The Shop in Grange*,

2013; No.23 *The Salute*, 2013; No.24 *Signpost*, 2013; No.25 *TEA*, 2013; No.26 *Raft Race*, 2013; No.27 *Blow-in*, 2014; No.28 *springs, pins & spirals, blades, hinges & nails, spikes & staples*, 2014; No.29 *BUS*, 2014; No.30 *The Cock's Step*, 2015; No.31 *I always have an audience 1*, 2015; No.32 *Abroad*, 2015; No.33 *Natural Cheese*, 2015; No.34 *Printing Shed*, 2015; No.35 *ABOVE*, 2016; No.36 *A Misplacement of Lichen*, 2016; No.37 *The Fermoy Pencil*, 2017; No.38 *I always have an audience 2*, 2019; No.39 *Distemper Brush*, 2019; No.40 *Knocklofty Bridge*, 2019.

I always have an audience for my work 2
Erica Van Horn, 2019 (Living Locally No.38)
16pp 150 x 105, digital, stapled.

Springs & Pins
Erica Van Horn, 2019
Print in folder, 180 x 240, digital in two colours, 24 copies.

Play Book
Maurice Scully, 2019
188pp 210 x 150, offset, casebound paper over boards.

Em & Me
Erica Van Horn, 2018
192pp 170 x 125, offset, paperback with 6 black & white images.

The Struggle of The Fly in Marmalade
Simon Cutts, 2018
Print in folder, 250 x 95, digital in four colours with rubber stamp fly and foil bocked cover, 50 copies.
After the stanza by W. B. Yeats, to whom it is dedicated.

Too Raucous For A Chorus
Erica Van Horn, with drawings by Laurie Clark, 2018
64pp 180 x 125, colour offset, casebound and blocked in two colours.

Cork City
Peter Downsbrough, 2017
60pp 155 x 230, offset, 300 copies.
Printed photographs made on the visit to Cork in 2011, to particpate in the 'In Other Words' exhibition at the Glucksman Gallery. This casebound book contains two maps of the city, and an embossed contact strip of the photographs set into the cover. The images convey the parallels and verticals of his photographs set in the sequence of book form, his usual medium.

a solution is in the room
Maud Cotter, 2017
25-panel concertina, 80 x 80, boxed 90 x 90 x 40, 100 copies.
A sculpture splayed out to a length of two metres on the floor when activated, using one letter of its title per panel.

Four Trees
Joan Roth, 2017
310 x 225, digital, casebound with embossed cover image, 100 numbered copies.

Birdsong
William Roth, 2017
176pp 170 x 125, offset, with cover photograph and frontispiece by Joan Roth.
Birdsong was written in the late-nineteen nineties, and is based almost entirely on incidents and characters from William Roth's life in Ireland. First published posthumously in 2015, this memorial edition is issued to celebrate the inauguration of the William and Joan Roth Lecture at the University of Limerick begining in April 2017. With postscript by Simon Cutts and Erica Van Horn of anecdotal jottings of lives unduly passsed over, and the contribution of William and Joan Roth to the life of the arts in Ireland over a period of more than sixty years.

Utility Building
Little Critic reprint, 2017
16pp 150 x 105, digital, stapled.
Photographs by Erica Van Horn of Ulrich Ruckreim's barn housing his sculptures in Clonegal on the border between Co. Carlow and Co. Wexford in Ireland. Half-size facsimile of *Little Critic Pamphlet 6*, December 1991.

Above
Erica Van Horn, 2016
24pp 230 x 170, letterpress in two colours, casebound, 250 numbered copies.
A collection of more of 'Living Locally', some seen as postcards, from the ongoing series which continues as a translation of the vernacular speech of where the author lives.

An Irish Potato Patch
2016
125 x 165, letterpress card in 2 colours on millboard.

The Tractor Run Plate
Erica Van Horn, 2016
210 diameter, 25 signed, numbered and boxed fired porcelain plates imitating the original paper plate.
"It began with a lot of old tractors being pulled out of barns and cleaned up for the day. A few of these machines get daily use as they are driven to and from the village for messages or Mass. Now there is a lot of excitement about seeing old tractors. Now they are called Vintage. Weeks are spent preparing and cleaning the tractors for The Tractor Run. I was trapped in the village this morning when the tractors set off, so I watched the entire procession as it lumbered away. I had no choice. The road was blocked. The Tractor Run headed to Ardfinnan. Its itinerary included a winding route back by way of other roads. The Run was long

and it was slow. There was no music. It was simply a ponderous, ungainly procession through country lanes. People at the few houses came out to wave. It was all being done for charity. It was for a good cause. Each year the Tractor Run has grown. Everyone wants to be involved. Shiny new tractors have joined in. Later, I found a paper plate with the number 27 written in black marker. There were two little holes in the center. Numbered paper plates had been tied with string into the radiator grill of each tractor."

A Misplacement of Lichen
Erica Van Horn, 2016
folded card 153 x 118, letterpress in plastic wallet, with fragment of lichen, 200 copies.
"From the route to Tullameghlan"

Natural Cheese
Erica Van Horn, 2015 (Living Locally No.33)
20pp 170 x 130, photocopy with letterpress, handsewn with wrappers.

My Ironmongery
Erica Van Horn, 2015
214pp 215 x 140, digital in two colours, stab-stitched with laminated wrappers, 100 numbered copies.
An inventory of many of the metal forms found and drawn by Erica Van Horn as a potential index of their acquisition and use and a hardware catalogue for further identification.

I always have an audience for my work
Erica Van Horn, 2015 (Living Locally No.38)
16pp 150 x 105, digital, stapled.
A second volume of almost identical photographs from the writer's studio door of the surrounding livestock who might anticipate her latest endeavours.

Raft Race
Postcard of a sign on the road to Newcastle, Co. Tipperary, September 2013, for the race on the River Suir, with the Knockmealdown Mountains in the distance. We heard reports of men and boys calling around to see people they had not visited in months. Everyone was looking for old plastic barrels with which to build their rafts. They were looking for plastic cladding, for large sheets of styrofoam or for some material which they had not thought of yet but which would help them stay afloat. The race was not so much about speed and arriving at the finish line as it was about not sinking. The small sign stayed up for several days after the race reminding us of what we had missed.

Living Locally
Erica Van Horn, Uniformbooks, 2014 (reprinted 2019)
144pp 234 x 142, offset in two colours, sewn paperback with flaps.

BUS
Erica Van Horn, 2014 (Living Locally No.29)
20pp 175 x 125, sewn with cover wrappers and label over print of current timetable for the Bus Eireann No.7 bus running from Cork to Dublin and vice versa, 200 copies.

for Bill Roth 1917–2014
Simon Cutts, 2014
Folded card 140 x 95, ink-jet marmalade print with rubber stamped fly, citing a stanza from W. B. Yeats' 'Wild Swans at Coole' of the year of Bill's birth.

TEA
Erica Van Horn, 2013 (Living Locally No.25)
16pp 150 x 105, digital, sewn in laminated cover, 300 copies. Short narratives on the subject, taken from the Journal and other sources, interspersed with drawings from *Nine Cups*.

Dubh
Coracle for STUDIOpractice 2011.
128pp 245 x 145, colour offset, casebound paper-over boards, 1000 copies.
An interspersing of contemporary Irish and America contemporary craft makers for an exhibition at the American Irish Historical Society in New York, October 2011. Foreword by Christopher Cahill, and an Introduction by Brian Kennedy, with the essays 'Darkness Be My Friend' by Marianne Mays and 'Tangled Up in Black' by Richard Deming to accompany work by twenty-nine makers.

Born in Clonmel
Erica Van Horn, 2011
20pp 145 x 105, photocopy with letterpress additions, sewn binding with wrappers, 200 copies.
A history of the scant presence of Laurence Sterne in the place of his birth, constituting Living Locally No 21 in the ongoing series.

Toscano
William Roth, 2011
8pp 145 x 105, photocopy with letterpress and tip-in, paper over boards in acetate pocket, edition of 95 copies with a few proofs. Short story about the last cigar always anticipated, on the occasion of the author's ninety-fifth birthday in September 2011.

8 Old Irish potatoes
Erica Van Horn & Simon Cutts, 2011
10-panel concertina in sleeve 90 x 90, offset in 2 colours. Describing: Snowdrop, Sackfiller, Lumper, Gawkies, Flourball, Home Guard, Up-to-Date and Snowflake. A sequel to the earlier *8 Old Irish Apples*.

MATERIALpoetry
Coracle for STUDIOpractice, 2011
96 pp 245 x 145, colour offset, casebound paper-over boards, 1000 copies.
An interspersing of contemporary Irish poets with the work of contemporary craft makers, for an exhibition at the American Irish Historical Society in New York, October and November 2010. Introduction by Christopher Cahill, with the essay 'Words and the makers', to accompany poems by Brian Coffey, Simon Cutts, Sean Dunne, Kit Fryatt, Vona Groarke, Michael Hartnett, Seamus Heaney, Trevor Joyce, Billy Mills, Eilean Ni Chuilleanain, Maurice Scully, Eithne Strong, Sheila Wingfield, and Augustus Young.

"If it can be done from here, it can be done anywhere" as it says here in the introduction. But that should also include the pervasive damp, the spasmodic couriers when not using the post office, parcels returned.

8 Old Irish apples
Erica Van Horn & Simon Cutts, 2008
8-panel concertina 90 x 90, letterpress, in acetate sleeve, 300 copies.
The names of eight Irish apples as a celebration of the work of Irish Seed Savers in Scariff, County Clare: Bloody Butcher, Eight Square Green, Chisel, Sheep's Snout, Mother of Household, Cabbage Stalk, No Surrender, Yellow Pitcher.

short-cuts
Erica Van Horn & Simon Cutts, 2008
8-panel concertina in sleeve 150 x 90, letterpress, 300 copies.

Folded Napkins
Erica Van Horn, 2008
16pp 150 x 110, two colour offset, hand-sewn, wrappers, 300 numbered copies.
"When we have guests staying for few days, I ask them to fold their napkins in a particular way so they will remember which one is theirs. Sometimes they remember and sometimes they forget, so I often make a drawing. Now I have acquired a collection of napkin drawings."

A little bit of butter
Edited by Peter Foynes for The Cork Butter Museum, 2007
48pp 125 x 173, offset and letterpress in seven colours, sewn casebound, 500 numbered copies.
A reprinting of some of the printing blocks used for butter wrappers by local creameries and agricultural co-ops, together with historical texts.

Gifts from the Government
Erica Van Horn, 2007
16pp 150 x 110, photocopy, offset, letterpress, laser colour copies and rubber stamps, sewn cover wrapper, 300 numbered copies.

Small Houses: The Buildings of Tom Browne
Erica Van Horn, 2007 (Living Locally No.12)
48pp 138 x 167, colour offset, casebound paper over boards, 500 copies.
"With age, Tom Browne has given up his building jobs. Now he works on small houses in his shed. He uses real building materials whenever possible, as these are the correct materials for houses. The houses he makes are builder's houses, made by a builder."

Numbers
Maurice Scully, 2006
Mounted print with six panels, 390 x 495, digital print with letterpress.

New Potatoes
Helen O'Leary & Paul Chidester, 2005
64pp 140 x 105, colour offset, spiral bound boards, 500 copies.
Attempts to decorate steel, concrete and stone with paintwork rarely last, but produce curious anachronisms for a time. This book journeys through the hardy, patchworked, yet dishevelled nature of the Irish countryside, from home in Leitrim to friends in Wexford, Roscommon and Mayo, via the boreens of Tipperary.

Forty Shades of Green
Edited by Brian Kennedy, Simon Cutts, Erica Van Horn, 2005
192pp 210 x 155, colour offset, casebound, 2500 copies.
A Convergence of Irish Art and Craft, for the Crafts Council of Ireland, with texts by Marianne Mays, Dermot Diamond and Eoin McNamee.

vinyl: project for installation
2005
108pp 160 x 150, colour offset, paperback, 1200 copies.
"The vinyl project used installations made of vinyl film as signs

and graphics output from the computer plotter and cutter. Vinyl was the single unifying means of making these works into a common medium, almost a theme of sorts."
Solveig Adalsteinsdottir, John Bevis, Boekie-Woekie, Christian Bok, Marie Bourget, Stephen Brandes, IYves Chaudouet, Thomas A. Clark, Susan Collis, Maud Cotter, Chris Drury, Matthew Falvey, Martina Galvin, Katie Holten, Susan Howe, Trevor Joyce, Cralan Kelder, Brian Kennedy, Caroline Koebel, Marton Koppany, Langlands & Bell, Billy Mills, Stuart Mills, Maurizio Nannucci, Mark Pawson, Kathy Prendergast, Tim Robinson, Kay Rosen, Colin Sackett, Eric Watier, Lawrence Weiner, Ian Whittlesea, Trevor Winkfield, Centre de Livres d'Artistes.

The Little Critic No.13
Tim Robinson 'Olwen Fouere & The Bull's Wall', 2004

Boats, Cots, Punts & Wherries
The Notebooks of Thomas Cuddihy, Piltown, Co. Kilkenny edited by Simon Cutts and with a Postscript, Bibliography and Glossary by Shay Hurley of The Workmen's Boat Club who initiated this project in 2004.
80pp 185 x 105, colour offset, casebound, 750 numbered copies.

Rusted
Erica Van Horn, 2004 (second edition of 150 copies 2007)
16pp 150 x 105, laser and letterpress in two colours, sewn with wrappers, 100 numbered copies.
Six small iron articles of unknown use found and drawn in Ballybeg.

Notional: Field Notes
Katie Holten, 2003 (with Butler Gallery Kilkenny)
76pp 170 x 140, offset with rubber stamps and tip-ins, printed endpapers and casebound paper over boards, 300 numbered copies.

Of Colour In Craft
Selected by Brian Kennedy, 2003
96pp 130 x145, colour offset , sewn paperback with flaps, 1500 copies (for the Crafts Council of Ireland).
The particular richness of contemporary craft-work in Ireland is shown here in detail by one of its aspects, the articulation and application of colour and material in the work of fourteen makers.

The Vegetable Plot at L8511
Tim Robinson, 2003
Print 445 x 310, colour offset with letterpress, 150 signed and numbered copies, in a water-tight mailing tube.
"In 1977 in the Aran Islands, M. and I tried our hands at growing vegetables for the first time, in a plot ridged like the traditional Aran potato field, beside our garden path. I kept the weather-beaten bit of paper recording our muddled efforts as a momento."

Kidnapped
Susan Howe, 2002
96pp 198 x 136, offset with five colour tip-ins, interleavings and bookmark, wrapper over casebinding, 300 signed and numbered copies.

Fredson Bowers & The Irish Wolfhound
J. C. C. Mays, 2002
84pp 190 x 140, colour offset with printed endpapers, casebound with embossed inlay, 500 copies.
Jim Mays suggests that Anglo-American bibliography would be different if Fredson Bowers had not passed over the distinctive features of the Irish book as he theorised his subject. "In the bucolic but still wild climes of South Tipperary, Fredson Bowers's wolfhound, ready defender of the flock of Anglo-American bibliographers, may meet up with another kind of wolf-hound, a dog crossbred with a wolf and ready to send the flock scattering" Marta Werner

Some Words For Living Locally
Erica Van Horn, 2002
12pp 147 x 105, letterpress in four colours, with rubber stamps, fingerprint ink and wrappers, 300 signed and numbered copies.
A facsimile of the Certificate of Registration under the Aliens Order of 1946.

The Money Jar
Erica Van Horn & Simon Cutts, 2002
40pp 160 x 115, colour offset with two-colour interleavings, casebound paper over boards, 500 copies.
"For many years the one pound jar has been the measure for making, and buying and selling jam and jelly. For thirty years the punt or pound has been the largest coin in the Irish currency: this book serves as a marking of the transition from punt to euro."

14 Blackthorns
Erica Van Horn and Simon Cutts, 1999
60pp 200 x 110, letterpress in two colours, casebound, 200 copies.
"a bundle found / in the soft floor / of the barn / tied with baling / twine & bound / for market"

15 Blackthorns
Erica Van Horn, 1999
Print 420 x 530, letterpress, 100 numbered copies.

The View from the Horizon
Tim Robinson, 1997
64pp 200 x 138, offset with five colour offset plates, sewn paperback with colour wrapper, 1000 copies.
A small anthology of the writings of Tim Robinson, together with a previously unpublished essay 'Geometer'.

Water of Recess
Simon Cutts & Erica Van Horn, 1993
Boxed glass flask of river water, 100 x 43 x 35, 30 copies.
"It was on a walk in Connemara while visiting the map-maker Tim Robinson in Roundstone, that we noticed the unevocatively named River Recess. We have been collecting the water of occasional rivers in a specimen case of glass tubes found some years earlier. With this river we emptied our drinking bottle and collected an entire litre. This small flask contains a fraction of it. Our thanks to Tim and Mairéad Robinson for tea with them and for the use of their map."

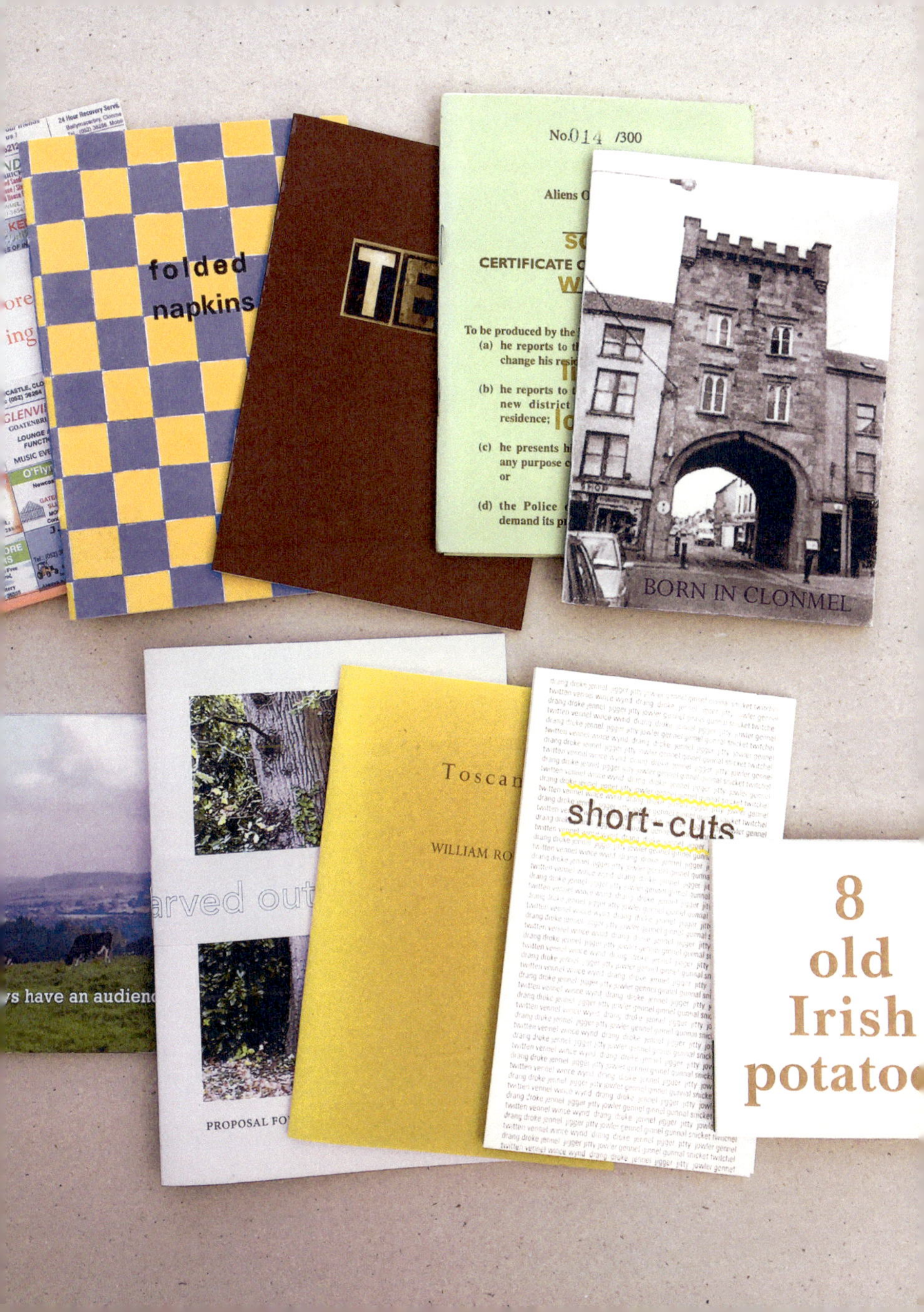

folded napkins
No.014 /300
Aliens O
CERTIFICATE O
To be produced by the
(a) he reports to t
change his resi
(b) he reports to t
new district
residence;
(c) he presents hi
any purpose o
or
(d) the Police
demand its p
BORN IN CLONMEL
Toscan
WILLIAM RO
arved out
ys have an audienc
PROPOSAL FO
Short-cuts
8
old
Irish
potato

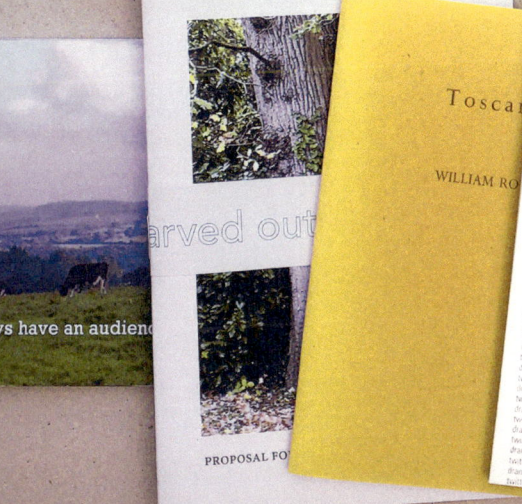

Frontispiece: *Water of Recess*, Simon Cutts & Erica Van Horn, Boxed glass flask of river water, 100 x 43 x 35, 30 copies, 1993.

p.28: Some of the plain, hardback and casebound books and sewn paperbacks, often with paper-over-boards photographic and blocked book cloth covers, in sizes barely changed from the octavo book—perhaps the first pocket book originating in Italy in the sixteenth century.

p.45: Some of the simpler small format and copy shop printed books, proposals, celebrations, at times part of series.

Endpapers: *The Irish harp is not constructed but carved out of a single tree like a canoe*, laminated paper tie on an ash tree of suitable girth.

An edition of 300 copies
Typesetting by Colin Sackett

ISBN 978-0-906630-67-9

University College Cork, Ireland
Coláiste na hOllscoile Corcaigh

Distributed in the UK, Europe and
Worldwide by Cornerhouse Publications
cornerhousepublications.org/books

Coracle
Ballybeg, Grange, Clonmel, Tipperary, Ireland
coracle.ie